W9-BBT-614

Date: 10/6/20

BR 796.334 PEL
Pelé,
For the love of soccer! /

PALM BEACH COUNTY
LIBRARY SYSTEM
3650 SUMMIT BLVD.
WEST PALM BEACH, FL 33406

BY **PELÉ**, THREE-TIME
WORLD CUP CHAMPION

ILLUSTRATED BY
Frank Morrison

Disney • Hyperion
LOS ANGELES NEW YORK

Ever since I was a little boy,

I knew soccer was the

game for me.

I would play with anyone,

anytime,

anywhere!

A few little taps or

one **big** kick—

I **loved** making the ball

do what I wanted it to do.

But practicing my moves

wasn't anything

compared to playing

in a real game.

When I was on the field, I was part of something special. I was part of the team.

The second
the starting whistle
blasted, every player
exploded into action.

Feet flying
over the turf,
we passed,
dribbled,
dodged.

And once the ball landed
in just the right spot . . .

I took my
best
shot!

There were times
when that ball
seemed to hang
in midair
forever,
until...

GO-O

-A-L-L!

You know what's better
than scoring in a
big game?
Nothing!

I've won a lot of games. Winning isn't everything, though—

being a **good sport** is what **really** counts.

Some people have called me the best soccer player in the world.
But I've never played for fame.

Pelé

I play for the
love
of the
game.

MORE ABOUT PELÉ

Pelé was born on October 23, 1940, in a small town in Brazil. His father, Dondinho, and his mother, Dona Celeste, named him Edson Arantes do Nascimento, but everyone called him Dico. He didn't get the nickname Pelé until he was nine or ten. To this day, he has no idea what "Pelé" means or who gave him the name. In fact, he didn't even like the nickname at first. But for some reason it stuck, so that's how he's known in the world today.

Soccer—or football, as he and people in many countries call it—was a big part of Pelé's life right from the start. His father played professionally until he hurt his knee.

He taught his son everything he knew. Dona Celeste, however, didn't want her boy to become a soccer player. She was afraid he'd hurt himself like his father had. In fact, she never attended one of Pelé's games, because she didn't want to see him get injured!

But Pelé loved the sport too much to give it up, even for his beloved mother.

Pelé grew up in a poor neighborhood. No one had money for soccer equipment. So he and his friends made balls out of old socks stuffed with newspapers. They played barefoot on dusty dirt roads. They formed a team and challenged other teams to matches. Some days they'd play soccer from dawn until dusk.

Pelé thought about soccer all the time. He daydreamed about it during school, even though he knew he'd be punished for not paying attention. He came up with schemes to make money to buy equipment. He collected and sold sports cards of famous soccer players. He shined shoes and boots.

It was a few years later, when he was fifteen, that Pelé was noticed by a famous soccer player named Waldemar de Brito. De Brito was so impressed that he helped Pelé sign up with his first professional team. The team was called Santos, after the town where it played.

Santos was far from Pelé's hometown, and at first he was very homesick. Once he packed his bags to take the train back to his family. But soon Pelé returned to the team. How could he do otherwise? Playing professional soccer was his dream, after all.

It was a dream he lived to the fullest. Pelé played for Santos from 1956 until 1974. During those years he also played on Brazil's National Team, helping them win three World Cups, the sport's top worldwide competition. He retired from Santos in 1974, but in 1975 joined a new team, the New York Cosmos.

Soccer wasn't a popular sport in the United States when Pelé first came to America. But thanks in large part to his amazing skills and personality, it soon gained a following that has grown by leaps and bounds. Today, boys and girls across the country play in leagues, in parks, and in their backyards.

Anyone who ever saw Pelé play knows that he was born to be a soccer player. His passion for the game shone through whenever he took to the field. And even today the magic of soccer, that beautiful game, shows in his wide smile when he dribbles or kicks a ball.

To the children of the world,
especially the children of America,
who received me with open arms when I
played for the New York Cosmos. —Pelé

For my home team: Nia,
Nyree, Tyreek, and Nasir.
Dream big! —F.M.

Text copyright © 2010 by Pelé
Illustrations copyright © 2010 by Frank Morrison

All rights reserved. Published by Disney • Hyperion, an imprint of Disney Book Group. No part of this book may be reproduced or transmitted in any form or by any means, electronic or mechanical, including photocopying, recording, or by any information storage and retrieval system, without written permission from the publisher. For information address Disney • Hyperion, 125 West End Avenue, New York, New York 10023.

Originally published in hardcover under the title *For the Love of Soccer!*, May 2010
First Hardcover Edition of *World of Reading: For the Love of Soccer!*, June 2020
First Paperback Edition of *World of Reading: For the Love of Soccer!*, June 2020
10 9 8 7 6 5 4 3 2 1
FAC-029261-20129
Printed in the United States of America

This book is set in Billy/SparkyType
Designed by David Hastings

Library of Congress Cataloging-in-Publication Control Number for *For the Love of Soccer!*
2009015890
Hardcover ISBN: 978-1-368-05629-8
Paperback ISBN: 978-1-368-05633-5

Reinforced binding on hardcover
Visit www.DisneyBooks.com